QUICK TIPS FROM THE

CBS
TENNIS
SPOT

QUICK TIPS FROM THE

CBS
TENNIS
SPOT

by Shep Campbell
Editor, Tennis Magazine

A
tennis
MAGAZINE
BOOK

Published by Golf Digest/Tennis Inc.,
A New York Times Company,
495 Westport Avenue
Norwalk, Connecticut 06856

Trade book distribution by
Simon and Schuster
A Division of Gulf + Western Industries, Inc.
New York, New York 10020

First Printing
ISBN: 0-914178-45-8
Library of Congress: 80-84952
Manufactured in the
United States of America

Cover and book design by Dorothy Geiser.
Typesetting by J&J Typesetters, Inc.
Norwalk, Connecticut
Printing and binding by Fairfield Graphics,
An Arcata Company

To Jennifer

PHOTO CREDITS

All photographs by Steve Szurlej except pages 11, 24, 99, 123, 130, 181, Michael Brent; 52, 56, John Newcomb; 73, Jay B. Siegel; 125, Henk Koster.

Front cover photo by Steven G. Sweitzer.

TABLE OF CONTENTS

INTRODUCTION

What's the one thing every tennis player is seeking? What do we all covet, even more than such pipe dreams as unlimited free court time or Rod Laver as a doubles partner?

Improvement, right? That is, the deep satisfaction of knowing we're getting better and approaching, however gradually, the real potential that we're sure is there.

That's the purpose of this book: to help you raise the level of your play and, thereby, get more fun out of the game. It does it a lot differently than the standard instruction book. Each page makes a concise, graphic point that's easy to remember and that you can apply immediately on the court. Collectively, moreover, these points add up to a thorough manual on how to play tennis better.

They have all been heard before, it should be noted. That's because they've been specially selected from the hundreds of 75-second "Tennis Spots" that I've been broadcasting every weekend since 1973—first on radio station WCBS-AM in New York City and for the past few years nationally on the CBS Radio Network. The text here is unchanged from the original scripts except for the removal of redundancies that are necessary on the airwaves, but not on the printed page, to emphasize the basic message.

As the Editor of TENNIS magazine, I draw all of the material for the "Tennis Spots" from the instruction articles in our publication. So I am indebted to the many talented

Tennis Magazine Editor Shep Campbell

people whose expertise and insights help create those articles. They contributed directly to this book, and they include:

Managing Editor Jeffrey Bairstow and Associate Editor Robert J. LaMarche; Instruction Advisory Board members Stan Smith, Tony Trabert, Vic Seixas, Ron Holmberg, Roy Emerson and Julie Anthony; Contributing Editors Arthur Ashe, Vic Braden, Allen Fox and Bob Harman; such stars as Bjorn Borg, Chris Evert Lloyd, Jimmy Connors and Billie Jean King; and the teaching professionals of the U.S. Professional Tennis Association.

Finally, the "Tennis Spots" would not have been possible without the generous guidance and cooperation of, among others, Lou Adler and Patsie Padula of WCBS-AM as well as Dick Brescia, Frank Miller, Dave Kurman, Ida Gianetta and Carol Preston of the CBS Radio Network.

All truly had a hand in this book and, thus, can share with you the credit for the improvement that's coming.

—Shep Campbell
Norwalk, Conn.
October, 1981

1.
GROUNDSTROKE
FUNDAMENTALS

FOCUS ON THE BALL

The most frequent command in tennis is, without question, the order to "watch the ball." But it isn't that easy to follow a moving ball, especially when you have so much else to think about on court and so many distractions.

Still, there are two things you can do which should pay off in smoother, sharper groundstrokes.

First, wait until you're just about to hit the ball to really focus on it intensely. If you try to concentrate completely on it from the moment it leaves your opponent's racquet, your mind may wander by the time you stroke the ball. So wait until the ball bounces on your side of the net before you really zero in on it.

Second, focus on something even smaller than the ball, Try to see if you can pick up its seams, for example. Using a small visual target that way helps you keep your eyes on the larger area of the ball.

So to watch the ball better, wait to concentrate really intently until it bounces, and then try to focus on one small area.

Gene Mayer

KEEP HEAD DOWN UNTIL FINISH

If too many of your groundstrokes wind up slapping into the net, there's a good possibility that you're watching the ball when you shouldn't be. I know that sounds like heresy, a violation of the most basic axiom in the game . . . the one about always keeping your eyes on the ball.

But there is one time when you shouldn't. That's at the moment when the ball comes off your racquet. At that moment, you should be keeping your head down, concentrating on the point where the racquet met the tennis ball.

The temptation is natural to lift your head to see where the ball is going, and maybe even to utter a prayer to help it over the net. But lifting your head will, ironically, have just the opposite effect. It will tend to keep the ball down and send it into the net.

That's because when you lift your head too soon, it makes you lift your racquet too soon, too. And that means you don't get a full swing at the ball.

Keep that head down until you've finished your stroke. Then, and only then, look up to see where your shot has gone.

GROUNDSTROKE FUNDAMENTALS

FOR LIGHT GRIP, HAVE A BIRD IN HAND

Many players are puzzled about just how firmly they should grasp the racquet. It may not seem to be all that critical a matter, but it is.

If you squeeze too hard, you'll tighten up your forearm and shoulder muscles, and that will prevent you from making a smooth, relaxed stroke. If you grip the handle too loosely, you won't be able to meet the ball firmly.

What's the right amount of pressure? It's to pretend that you have a bird in hand. In other words, to imagine that the racquet in your hand is a live bird. You want to hold it firmly enough so that it won't escape. But you don't want to grasp it so hard that you'll crush it.

That's the key to gripping a racquet. With that amount of pressure, you won't be holding it so loosely that it will slip out of your hand. Yet your forearm and shoulder muscles will be relaxed enough so that you can make a flowing, forward swing.

Arthur Ashe

KEEP YOUR FEET MOVING

If there's one thing most pros agree on, it's that a player is only as good as his or her footwork. You can have the most fantastic strokes in the world. But they won't do you much good if you don't move well on the court.

The secret to good footwork is always to keep your feet moving. Never let them fall asleep on the court.

Try to stay on the balls of your feet as you watch your opponent go for the ball to make his shot. And try to anticipate as soon as you can where he's going to send the ball so that you can start moving toward that spot.

Even as great a champion as Arthur Ashe will tell you that he used to write notes to remind himself to keep his feet moving. And he left the notes on the sideline where he'd see them between the games in a match.

Of course, the ability to move well on court won't do you much good if you have lousy strokes. All it will do is give you more time to hit a crummy shot. But remember that a player is generally only as good as his footwork. So to get the most from your strokes, keep those feet moving.

PUT YOUR BEST FOOT FORWARD

There can be many reasons for flubbing a shot, but one of the most common is hitting the ball off the wrong foot.

Fortunately, it's easy to correct that problem . . . if you follow two rules for body positioning.

Rule No. 1 is to wait for every shot with your body facing the net. Many players tend to get lazy after they hit the ball. They just stay where they are to watch what the opponent is doing.

Instead, you must hop back so that your shoulders are parallel to the net and you're in position to turn quickly to either side for the next shot. Otherwise, you won't get to it on time . . . or with your body properly balanced.

Rule No. 2 is to hit every groundstroke with your body sideways to the net. Many players tend to hit the ball with their bodies nearly facing the net because that takes less footwork. But it also means they are getting less weight into their shots.

So put your best foot forward on the court. Make sure you're facing the net when you're waiting for shots, and are sideways to the net when you're hitting them.

USE YOUR FREE HAND TO PREPARE

Driving a car with only one hand on the wheel can be both tiring and dangerous. In the same sense, using only one hand to guide your racquet when you're preparing for a groundstroke, can be tiring—and dangerous, too— dangerous, at least, to your success in hitting the ball right.

You should always keep two hands on your racquet when you're in the ready position waiting for the ball, and when you take the racquet back to hit a forehand or backhand. You should have your stroking hand on the handle and your other, free hand cradling the racquet at the throat.

There are two reasons for that. First, you can use your free hand to help you rotate the racquet for the proper grip. And second, you can use your free hand to start pushing your racquet back as you begin the backswing. That will force you to turn your upper body and shoulders the way you should to prepare for the shot. Then, let go of the racquet with your free hand when it feels natural.

Prepare for a groundstroke the way you should drive a car . . . with both hands on the wheel.

Chris Evert Lloyd

GRUNT!
FOR MORE POWER

Among today's top players, Jimmy Connors punctuates his shots with a big grunt. John McEnroe has a kind of groan. And Chris Evert Lloyd emits a more lady-like wheeze when she hits the ball.

These sound effects on court are not just some fad. Tennis players have discovered what those in the martial arts have known for a long time: that grunting equals power.

In a sport like karate, for example, a performer usually shouts when he chops through a board. What that does is contract the stomach muscles at the moment of impact and make it possible to put more force into the motion.

The same principle applies when a tennis player grunts as he hits the ball.

Beyond that, many players say grunting helps their concentration because they've got to time the grunt and the hit.

So why not try grunting the next time you're on the court? You may be a bit embarrassed at first. But you'll probably get over it quickly . . . because there's nothing embarrassing about hitting the ball better.

MEET THE BALL EARLY

There's one simple playing characteristic that seems to distinguish the great players of the world from the good players, and the good ones from the average players. And that is how far out in front they meet the ball.

Letting the ball come right up to you before you make contact with your groundstrokes can cost you dearly in accuracy, power and control on the court. Indeed, it's only the poor tennis player who lets the ball get to his side before he hits it.

Go out after the ball instead of waiting for it to come to you. Start your backswing well before the ball is upon you . . . even before it crosses the net. Inches count here, remember, and the farther out in front you are able to meet the ball, the greater your chances will be of making a good shot.

THROW YOUR WEIGHT AROUND

There's one time when you definitely want to throw your weight around a bit. And that's when you're about to hit a groundstroke.

Some players have a tendency to hit the ball while their weight is still on the back foot. And others hit the ball after their weight has already transferred to the forward foot. In both cases, they lose a lot in terms of power and control.

What you should do is try to hit the ball while your weight is shifting forward. You can use this weight to add strength and direction to the stroke.

If you're hitting a lot of shots while your weight is still back, the chances are that you're not anticipating the ball properly. You're getting caught hitting the ball after it's already started to sink.

The best cure for this problem is to try to take the oncoming ball on the rise. That will automatically encourage you to shift your weight forward as you bring the racquet into and through the ball.

If you're hitting the ball after your weight has already shifted forward, you're probably not moving your feet into position correctly. Try to be more nimble on your feet, and you should find that you're getting to the ball sooner.

Guillermo Villas

SWING LOW
TO HIGH
FOR TOPSPIN

There are few players in the world who can outlast Guillermo Vilas in a rally from baseline to baseline.

What's the key to Vilas' success? He says it's the topspin he puts on the ball.

Topspin gives the ball a forward rotation that does two things. It pulls the ball down quickly into the court. And after it lands, the ball kicks high and deep behind the baseline.

That accomplishes Vilas' main purpose: keeping his opponent pinned deep in his court where he can't attack . . . and probably can't out-rally Vilas.

How do you hit a topspin ball like Vilas'? He says there are two keys. First, start your forward swing below the spot where you want to meet the ball. Then, swing up and forward to bring the racquet strings up the back of the ball. That's what produces the topspin.

One other thing: the farther out in front of you that you meet the ball, Vilas adds, the greater the topspin you'll produce.

IGNORE APPEARANCES ON TOPSPIN

Topspin is all the rage these days, popularized by such stars as Bjorn Borg and Guillermo Vilas. So you see lots of club players trying to roll their racquets over the ball because it looks like that's the way the pros get topspin.

But it isn't. It's physically impossible to come up and over the ball at impact and still hit it over the net.

The ball is on the strings of a racquet for a fraction of a second . . . which means that even if you were able to get your racquet face over the top of the ball at impact, the best you could do is hit yourself in the foot.

Sure, it looks like some of the top pros hit topspin by bringing their racquets over the top of the ball. But actually, their wrists are fixed at impact. The roll-over that looks so great doesn't really occur until long after the ball has left the strings.

The way the pros hit topspin . . . and the way you can, too . . . is to keep the wrist firm and to swing from low to high. In other words, bring your racquet up to meet the ball and keep the face of the racquet vertical at impact. Then, if you want to roll it over, fine.

Anyone, even a guy who trips over the baseline, can learn to hit topspin. Just forget about rolling the racquet over the ball, and bring it from low to high.

GROUNDSTROKE FUNDAMENTALS

HIT ALL SHOTS WAIST-HIGH

Unlike a golf ball, which sits there conveniently at a player's feet on every shot, a tennis ball arrives at a different speed— and at a different height—on almost every shot. Sometimes it sails up high, sometimes it skips low and sometimes it hardly bounces at all.

But if at all possible, you should hit every forehand or backhand at the same height . . . that is, at waist level. That's the way to get the most power and control into every shot.

It takes some practice to acquire the habit of always taking groundstrokes at waist level. You have to learn to back-pedal for high, bouncing balls, and to come up and bend down for the short ones.

But a good way to learn is to go out on a court without your racquet and have someone hit balls at you. Try to catch each one of them in your hands at waist height. It's sometimes easier to get a habit like this one ingrained in your mind if you don't have to concentrate on hitting the ball, too.

Hitting every forehand and backhand that you possibly can at waist level is the key to solid, consistent groundstrokes.

PUSH, DON'T PULL

Did you ever notice how much easier it is to push a door open than it is to pull it open? Or to push a heavy object, rather than to pull it?

Well, the same principle applies when you play tennis . . . especially on groundstrokes.

It's easy to push a ball on a forehand or backhand stroke because your wrist and your weight are behind the racquet. But it's hard to pull a racquet through the ball because your hand and body weight are ahead of the contact point. All you can do to get the ball back is to muscle the shot.

There are two simple ways to make sure that you're pushing, and not pulling, your shots.

The first is to check to see that you are using the proper Eastern forehand or backhand grips. Each grip puts the bulk of your hand and wrist behind the racquet handle where it belongs.

The second way is to meet the ball out in front of your forward foot. If you meet the ball early enough, it's easy to push your weight through the shot.

2.
FOREHANDS
AND BACKHANDS

PUT POWER BEHIND THE BALL

New York's Vitas Gerulaitis is known as a playboy. They call him Broadway Vitas . . . and not without reason. But he's also known as the owner of one of the most lethal forehands in the men's pro game.

Gerulaitis says there are three keys to his success with the forehand. And those three keys are simple and easy to remember.

First, take your racquet back as early as possible. If you do that, you'll not only get yourself positioned properly for the shot, you also won't have to rush your swing, which is the cause of so many errors by club players.

Second, always be sure to bend your knees. If they're stiff, you can't move into the ball the way you should. And, of course, you can't get down for low balls.

Finally, follow through completely on your forehands. That's essential for control.

Remember Broadway Vitas' three keys to success with the forehand. Take your racquet back early. Bend those knees. And follow through completely. You may wind up in the spotlight, too.

Vitas Gerulaitis

IRON OUT
YOUR FOREHANDS

If your forehands fly around the court like a deranged starling, there's an easy way to correct the problem: pretend you're ironing the ball.

The reason your shots are so inconsistent is that you lack a smooth, steady swinging motion, with a good, long follow-through.

One way to develop that nice, long swing is to imagine that your racquet is moving along the top of an ironing board as you swing. Pretend that the ball is sitting on top of the ironing board, and that you're trying to sweep it off.

That does a couple of things. First, it guarantees that you'll meet the ball with a smooth, level swing every time. You'll be hitting through the ball, the way you should.

And second, by continuing your swing along the plane of the ironing board, you'll be sure you finish the stroke with a complete follow-through. That's what gives you the control you need.

So use that ironing board to iron out your forehand problems.

USE YOUR PALMS TO SQUARE UP SHOTS

Players who have trouble hitting their forehands squarely usually don't understand how the racquet face and the ball should be aligned at impact.

The correct alignment is perfectly square, with racquet head perpendicular to the ground and racquet strings facing in the direction you want the ball to go.

If the racquet face is closed, or facing slightly toward the ground, the ball will tend to go into the net. If the face is open, or facing slightly skyward, the ball will tend to fly long.

A good way to develop a feeling for square contact on your forehands is to think of hitting the ball with the open palm of your hand . . . almost as though you were playing handball rather than tennis. The palm would have to be held perpendicular to the ground for you to hit the ball properly. And that's the position you want your racquet in, too.

If you've been having trouble hitting the ball squarely on your forehands, imagine that you are trying to slap through it with the palm of your hand. That will get your racquet face squared up at impact and send your forehands sailing over the net, the way they should.

BRUSH YOUR CHIN

If you're going to hit a forehand with consistency and control, you've got to bring your racquet up into a full follow-through after you hit the ball.

Most players realize that. But they sometimes forget it under the pressure of playing a match. Their arm and shoulder muscles tighten up. And that produces a short, abrupt follow-through . . . which makes it really tough to control the ball.

To get the full follow-through you need to control a forehand, you should always do one thing. And that is bring your hitting shoulder up so that it brushes your chin after you hit the ball.

That accomplishes several things. It gives you a smooth, loose swing. It guarantees that you'll bring the racquet up as high as you should for a full follow-through. And it means you'll have your racquet properly positioned to send the ball where you want it to go.

So if your forehands aren't as accurate as you'd like, you're probably not following through the way you should. Begin bringing your hitting shoulder up to brush your chin after you hit the ball.

Ivan Lendl

CATCH
RACQUET ON
FOLLOW-THROUGH

Do too many of your forehands lack control? Do too many of them fall short, where your opponent can easily jump on them?

You've got a follow-through problem. And a good way to correct it is to practice catching your racquet in your free hand as you finish the shot. That will automatically extend your stroke and also improve your overall balance when you hit a forehand.

Be sure to stretch both your arms out at shoulder level after you've hit the ball. Your shoulder on your racquet side should finish up under your chin. At the same time, you should be able to catch the racquet with your free hand.

You can't quit early on the forehand stroke. If you do, you'll sacrifice both control and depth. To catch the ball right, practice catching your racquet in your free hand on your follow-through.

TOSS A FRISBEE

Most top players consider the backhand an easier stroke than the forehand. A lot of club players can't understand that. The reason is that, unlike the pros, they don't hit backhands with a natural motion.

One good way to get a feeling for that flowing natural motion is to think of tossing a Frisbee, or a pie plate, through the air.

Remember how you throw a Frisbee? You stand sideways to the target, draw your arm back close to your body and then swing forward until your arm straightens out naturally. That's exactly the motion you're after with a backhand.

Use this uncoiling action of the Frisbee throw with your backhand stroke. You'll find that it will help you keep your elbow close to your body and help you bring your racquet through the ball . . . the way you should.

With this Frisbee motion, you may be surprised by how easy—and effective—a backhand can be.

HIT A TWO-HANDER LIKE A BASEBALL SLUGGER

You wouldn't think that little Tracy Austin has much in common with a big baseball player like George Brett. But she does, in at least one important way.

She hits her most lethal shot, her two-handed backhand, just the way Brett hits a baseball. And almost as hard, believe me.

If you use the two-handed backhand, or would like to try it, keep that image in mind the next time you're on the court.

Get ready for the shot with your feet roughly parallel to the flight of the ball. Bend your knees and draw your racquet back, the way a baseball hitter does when a pitch is coming.

Then, as the ball arrives, pivot your hips and really rip into it. This is the critical part in hitting a two-handed backhand, just as it is in hitting a baseball. Put your full weight behind your swing and meet the ball out in front of you before following through.

To hit a two-handed backhand the way Tracy Austin does, pretend you're swinging a bat the way George Brett does. You should get some big-league results.

Tracy Austin

BEAT A RUG

The key to a solid and consistent backhand stroke is always to hit through the ball at impact . . . that is, to try to keep the ball on the strings of your racquet for as long as possible. That'll assure you of making a full, fluid swing.

An easy way to get the feel for hitting through the ball is to imagine using your racquet to beat a rug that's hanging on a clothesline.

To do a good job of that, your front shoulder, arm, wrist, and racquet would all have to be lined up and touching the rug as you hit it. That's what would enable you to hit the rug the hardest and pound the most dust out of it.

That's precisely the same position you should be in on the court when you're meeting the ball for a backhand.

To beat any backhand problem you may have, pretend that you're beating a hanging rug.

TUCK A BALL
UNDER YOUR ARM

The backhand seems to give more average players more grief than any other stroke. If you've had more than your share of that grief, try this little trick the next time you practice. Take a spare ball and tuck it under your upper arm next to your body.

That will force you to keep your elbow close to your body, where it should be on the backswing.

The reason so many players are erratic on the backhand is that they hit the ball too far away from their bodies. And that robs them of power and control. Instead, you should use a compact backswing, keeping your arm flexed and your elbow close to your body. It should be only two or three inches away.

To be sure that it is, try the device of tucking a ball under your upper arm. If the ball falls out during your backswing, it means that you're straightening your arm too much. You're hitting the ball too far away from your body.

The spare ball should fall to the court only when you bring your racquet forward to meet the ball. By then, you'll have your racquet positioned for the kind of consistent backhand you're after.

PRETEND YOU'RE IN A TUG-OF-WAR

Is your backhand as reliable as a politician's promise? If it is, the reason may be that you're not shifting your weight into the shot.

A simple way to overcome that problem is to imagine, during the forward swing, that you are involved in a tug-of-war with your own racquet.

Pretend that the racquet handle is the rope, and you'll automatically lean foward, pushing your weight off your back foot and into the stroke where it belongs.

This tug-of-war action will also help you keep your elbow straight and close to your body. That way, you'll hit through the ball, rather than just slap at it with a feeble, wristy motion.

So play tug-of-war on your backhand by pulling on the handle of your racquet as though it were the rope when you move to the ball.

That will help you transfer your weight as you make your forward swing. And you should find that your backhand, which had been a disaster area, can be the source of many a triumph out on the court.

3.
SERVING/
RETURNING

Andrea Jaeger

REACH UP AND OUT

It's vital to reach up and out for the ball when you hit a serve. That's what puts some punch into it.

One way to visualize that reaching motion is to think of how a javelin thrower hurls his spear at a track meet. You've probably noticed that at the instant he releases the javelin, he extends his body fully in the process. It's this extension, together with his forward movement and the uncoiling of his body, that allows him to transfer all of his power into his throw.

When you serve, of course, you don't enjoy the same kind of running start that a javelin thrower does. But at the critical moment . . . the moment you hit the ball . . . you should reach up and out, just the way a javelin thrower does, at the moment of release.

If you extend yourself just a few inches to make contact with the ball, you'll hit your serves with more power, depth and accuracy.

USE THE COUNTDOWN SYSTEM

Some players have a problem serving because they don't know how to coordinate the twin actions of releasing the ball and then hitting it.

A good way to learn to blend these two actions is to practice the serve according to a count of THREE.

You should start out with both arms held out in front of you about chest high. On the count of ONE, both your arms should go down. That is, the arm with the racquet and the arm with the ball should both drop at the same rate of speed.

On the count of TWO, your ball arm should come up in front of you and your racquet arm should come up behind you. This point in the service motion is like a bird spreading its wings.

On the count of THREE, your racquet should come forward to hit the ball at the peak of its rise.

By counting down as you practice the serve, you're sure to develop a smoother motion. Count ONE for the drop of the arms, TWO for the lift of the arms, and THREE for the hit.

THROW YOUR RACQUET

If you're having trouble getting your serve over the net, there's one simple thing you can do in practice to help correct the problem. And that is to throw your racquet over the net.

The root of your problem is that you're either pulling your head down as you meet the ball, or pulling your racquet down . . . or both.

It's an easy habit to break. All you have to do to develop the proper motion is to go out on a court and practice actually throwing an old racquet over the net.

On your first few throws, you'll probably find that the racquet will hit the ground in front of the net. But keep at it. Throw the racquet up and out. Before long, you'll find that the racquet is sailing comfortably over the net.

That's the motion you need when you're serving for real. It will help you to keep your head up and your racquet extended through contact, so your serves will clear the net.

Jimmy Connors

DEVELOP
A ROUTINE

If you get a chance to watch Jimmy Connors in action at a tournament, observe what he does right before every serve. It could be a big help to your game.

Connors bounces the ball four times before he serves. You don't necessarily need to bounce the tennis ball four times. A couple of times will do. But doing that can accomplish two important things for you.

First, it builds concentration for the serve by taking your mind off the last point and bringing it to bear on the important one that's coming up.

Second, it forces you to lean forward and get your weight onto your front foot. That sets you up for the proper weight shift on the serve.

Take a moment, as Connors does, to bounce the tennis ball once or twice before you serve. It helps your concentration. And it prepares your body for the proper kind of weight shift.

TOSS THE BALL
27 INCHES

When you toss the ball for the serve, you should lift it about 27 inches above your outstretched hand. That's the height where you'll meet it with your racquet.

Too many club players, though, think they need extra time to coordinate the toss with the hit. So they'll toss the ball so high that it seems to take a half hour to come down. And that's destroyed more good serves than almost anything else.

The worst part of tossing the ball too high is that you have to wait for it to drop. That means that somewhere along the line you have to put on the brakes by slowing down either your racquet or your body motion. And that destroys any semblance of a smooth serving motion.

On top of that, a high toss may give you more time to prepare for a big effort. But it really gives you less time to make good contact because the ball is falling so much faster when you try to hit it.

So remember. You really only need to toss the ball about 27 inches above your out-stretched hand.

That might not seem like much of a toss. But it's all that the great servers have ever needed. They hit the ball at that precise instant when it stops rising and seems to hang motionless in space. In other words, when it's a perfect target.

KEEP THE TOSSING ARM HIGH

Most players rarely think about it. But when you're serving, the position of your non-racquet arm after you've tossed the ball can be critical.

What you should do with that other arm is keep it up. The natural tendency is to let it drop in order to get it out of the way as the racquet swings over your shoulder to meet the ball.

But you've got to fight that tendency.

If you drop your non-racquet arm after your toss, you'll pull your body down with it. You'll cramp your swing and, very probably, meet the ball sooner than you should, sending it into the net.

But if you keep your non-racquet arm up, you'll avoid that. And there will be other benefits, too. For one thing, it will help you keep your eyes on the ball, which is absolutely vital. It's hard to look down when both your arms are pointing up.

Keep your non-racquet arm up after it's released the ball when you serve. It won't get in your way. In fact, it will do a lot to help you get your way on your serves.

Stan Smith

ROTATE SHOULDERS FOR MORE POWER

At the clinics where he works with average players, Stan Smith has noticed one especially common mistake on the serve. And that's a failure to rotate the shoulders.

Too many club players serve with their shoulders square to the net. That means the burden of putting power behind the ball falls entirely on the arm and wrist. And it's impossible, Smith says, to generate any real speed that way.

To get that speed, you should rotate your shoulders smoothly as you move your racquet up to meet the ball.

It's not hard to develop that shoulder rotation . . . if you remember one thing. Keep your front arm pointing up in the air a little longer after your ball toss.

That way, your shoulders will be roughly at right angles to the net as you start bringing your racquet up. And you'll have to rotate your shoulders forward in order to hit the ball. That simple action, Smith says, will give you the power you want.

ANCHOR YOUR FRONT FOOT

A lot of club players wind up for the serve as if they're drum majors leading a parade down Main Street. All that this wasted motion does is make it more difficult for them to get the ball in.

But it's easy to keep the serving motion simple and compact . . . and, therefore, more effective. The key is to keep your front foot anchored to the court from the moment you begin to serve.

A lot of players don't realize that. They put a lot of surplus motion into their preparation for the serve. The trouble with that is it keeps you from shifting your weight forward onto your front foot as your racquet makes contact with the ball. That timing is the major source of power on the serve.

The easiest way to have your weight on your front foot when you hit a serve is to keep it there from the start.

So try to think of that front foot as being anchored or glued to the court as you begin the serve. Let your weight remain on your front foot as you take the racquet back. Then, during the forward swing, let your back foot swing into the court past the anchored front foot.

Forget about fancy windups on your serves. If you're like most players, you'll serve with more power by anchoring your weight on your front foot from the start . . . and keeping it there until you've hit the ball.

SWING AN AXE TO SLICE THE BALL

You can't have a solid game if you lack a dependable slice serve. And developing one may be easier than you realize. Just think of swinging the racquet the way you'd swing an axe over your head.

The slice serve should be hit with a brushing motion. That's what puts the spin on the ball, pulling it down safely in your opponent's court where it then veers off to the side.

The key to getting that spin on the slice serve is to snap your wrist as you meet the ball. That does two things. First, it gives extra acceleration to the racquet just before impact. And second, it imparts the brushing motion to the ball that you want.

Some players have trouble mastering the wrist snap. But if you think of the action as just like the one you'd use . . . if you were throwing an axe end over end toward the net . . . you'll find that's just the motion you need to hit a slice serve.

PITCH YOUR SERVES

Roscoe Tanner, the fastest server in tennis, has a lot more in common with Nolan Ryan, the fastest pitcher in baseball, than you might suspect.

If you stop to think about it, the arm motion used to serve in tennis is identical to the motion a pitcher uses to throw a baseball. In fact, since most men have had a lot more experience throwing baseballs than women, that may be one reason their serves are generally better.

If your serve is giving you trouble, one good way to get the proper motion for it is to spend some time throwing a tennis ball the way a pitcher throws a baseball.

The key lies in the wrist snap. That's what allows a baseball pitcher to put something on the ball, and also to throw curves. It's the same with the serve in tennis. A wrist snap, just as your racquet meets the ball, is what gives your serve some zip, and also allows you to put some spin on the ball.

As you snap your wrist, you can rotate your palm slightly to help you aim the ball with your racquet. The ball will go in the direction that your palm is pointing.

Roscoe Tanner

MAKE THE FIRST SERVE GOOD

There's one very obvious, and inescapable, statistic that far too many players ignore: those who get 60 to 70 percent of their first serves in are the ones who win most of the matches.

Many men players, in particular, insist on hitting serves with all the power they can. They'll overlook their many double faults or weak second serves if they can just manage to zing in a few cannonballs during every match. Winning one point with a macho ace seems to mean more than winning five points by serving carefully.

Many women players, on the other hand, get too crafty when serving. They try to place first serves on the lines or in the corners. They'll catch an opponent off guard this way on some serves. But they'll miss so many others that a smart opponent will still have the upper hand.

To get more of your first serves in, don't try for quite so much power or precision. Ease up. Concentrate on smoothness rather than speed, and keep the ball more toward the center of the service box.

Aim to get 60 to 70 percent of your first serves in and watch your winning percentage climb.

STRENGTHEN YOUR SECOND SERVE

Playing the game with a weak second serve is like driving a car without a spare tire. You're just inviting trouble.

A reliable second serve will strengthen your game in two ways.

First, it'll make you less tense about your first serve because that one won't seem so all-important. You'll be more relaxed. And because of that, you'll be more likely to hit it well.

Second, a reliable second serve will give you a psychological edge. Your opponent won't get the lift that comes when he sees your first serve misfire and he knows that he can then count on a lame second serve.

Too many players concentrate solely on their first serves, with the result that their second serves come across the net like creampuffs . . . if they come across at all. Work on the second serve. Stop inviting trouble for yourself.

HOP ON THOSE RETURNS

The reason many players have problems returning serve is simply that they're not ready for the ball.

One way to make sure you're ready, and to get an early start on the shot, is to hop lightly in the air the moment you see the ball leave the server's racquet. This hop will accomplish two things for you.

First, it helps rid your body of tension and allows you to move your racquet back more quickly for a proper backswing.

Second, it gets you on your toes so that you're in a better position to move to either side to retrieve the ball.

Don't get caught sleeping on the return of serve. Remember to hop lightly the moment the ball leaves the server's racquet.

Virginia Wade

HANG IN FOR HAPPIER RETURNS

Almost every tennis player recognizes that the serve is the most important shot in the game. But do you know which is the second most important?

It's the return of serve . . . the shot every player has to hit on half of all the points he plays. Yet, as important as it is, the return of serve is rarely practiced and, as a result, seldom hit as well as it could be by most club players.

It isn't hard to return serves well, though, even if they do come at you with a lot of speed or spin on the ball. Just remember two key things.

First, against a reasonably good server, stand several feet behind the baseline on the first serve. Then, on the second serve, move up to the baseline or just inside it. Get in a semi-crouch position with your knees bent and your weight forward. Hold the racquet with both hands out in front of you, so that you're ready for either a forehand or a backhand shot.

Second, watch the ball from the moment the server begins his toss. For some reason, many players find it harder to follow the ball when they're returning serve than at any other time. Maybe the server's motion distracts them. Maybe they're worrying about whether he'll charge the net.

Forget about all of that. Keep in mind that if your eye is on the ball, your return of serve will be, too.

PREPARE FOR CANNONBALLS

What can you do when you face a player who hits serves that seem to come out of a bazooka?

Returning effectively against a hard server depends on two things: preparation and a shorter backswing.

The key to preparation is to make sure you're properly set for the serve, and to watch the ball intently from the time it leaves the server's hand. That way, you can determine where the ball will be coming as soon as possible after the server hits it.

Once you see that, get your racquet back as quickly as you can. Against fast serves, there isn't enough time to make a full backswing. You'll have to shorten it and just concentrate on hitting through the ball. As a rule of thumb, your racquet should have reached the limit of its backswing as the server's ball crosses the net.

Remember, you can use the speed on a hard serve to hit a hard return yourself. But it all depends on preparing for the shot properly and shortening your backswing.

PLAN YOUR RETURNS

One of the most common mistakes many players make on the return of serve is to try to play the ball on impulse. They'll wait until the last second to decide where they're going to hit it. And then they'll wonder why they don't score better with their returns.

The server has enough of an advantage on each point. Why give him more? To improve your chances against him, make up your mind what you're going to do with each serve as you wait for the ball. Then stick to that decision.

Generally, it's smart to go crosscourt on the return of serve, trying to hit deep to the opposite corner of the court. You're going across the lower part of the net that way. And you have more court to hit into with the ball.

But whatever choice you make, have a plan in mind for your returns of serve. And stick to it. There isn't enough time to make a sound decision in the split second you have after the ball arrives . . . especially if you're facing somebody with a scorching serve.

4.
NET PLAY

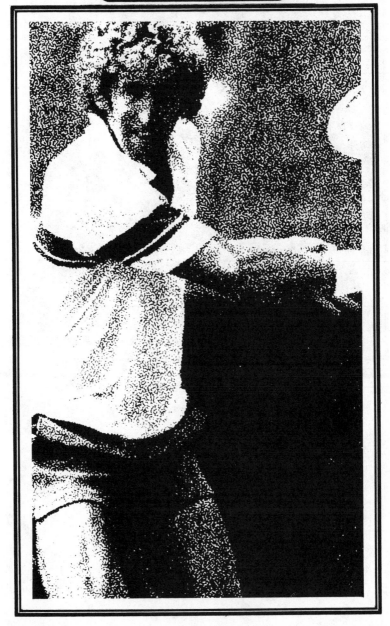

Brian Gottfried

SHORTEN STROKE TO HIT APPROACH

The approach shot is sometimes called a transportation shot because it's used to transport you from the baseline up to the net.

There are two things in particular that you should remember when you hit an approach shot.

The first is use your best stroke. If you normally are successful with a flat backhand, for example, go with that stroke. This isn't a time to get fancy or to take chances on the court. Use your most reliable weapon.

Second, shorten your backswing on the approach shot . . . whichever stroke you use. There's no need for a full backswing as there is on a conventional groundstroke because you won't have to hit the ball the full length of the court.

So approach the approach shot with your best ground-stroke and a short backswing.

GO TO NET
WITHOUT FEAR

In any match, but particularly in doubles, you've got to get to the net at least some of the time in order to win.

Some players, though, are afraid of the net. The way to overcome that fear is to remember two basic facts.

First, you can easily catch with your hands any ball hit to you at the net. And if you can catch it, the odds are that you can certainly hit it.

Second, your racquet doesn't have to be moved as far at the net as it does in the backcourt. So you can protect yourself better if it comes to that.

One way to conquer a fear of the net is to stand up there and practice stop volleys . . . that is, shots that barely drop over the net. Have another player hit balls to you while you simply cup your hand around the racquet handle and just let the approaching ball bounce off the strings.

It's true, of course, that you have less time to react to the ball when you're at the net than when you're in the backcourt. But you also don't have to move the racquet as far.

So get over that fear of the net. Get up there . . . and put a little fear into the other guy.

KEEP YOUR BACK TO THE WALL

No one likes to have his back to the wall in tennis. But there is one time when you want to . . . figuratively speaking, that is. And that's when you're volleying up at the net.

You should imagine your back is to the wall when you volley because that will help you to remember the one thing that's the key to the stroke: a short, compact backswing.

The volley should be hit with a punching motion that employs little or no backswing. There isn't time for a big backswing when you're up at the net. The ball comes at you too fast. And if you take the racquet back as you do for other strokes, the ball will probably shoot past you before you can hit it. Or at best, you'll make a weak shot.

To help you shorten your backswing, pretend that your back is against that imaginary wall. That will prevent you from taking your racquet too far back behind your shoulder. And it will force you to use the punching motion that you should on volleys.

So get your back to the wall on volleys. That way, you'll avoid really getting your back to the wall in a match.

John McEnroe

BEND FOR LOW VOLLEYS

One big, yet simple, thing that helped carry John McEnroe to the top of the sport was a pointer he once received on volleying.

"I used to be very lazy on my low volleys," he recalls. "I didn't get down for them. I just bent at the waist. That meant I had to drop the head of my racquet and scoop the ball back. And that gave my opponents easy, rising balls they could jump on."

Now, McEnroe bends his knees sharply for low volleys. The big advantage of getting down low is that it allows you to keep the head of your racquet above the level of your wrist. That means you can swing through the ball, the way you should, and send it skimming low over the net.

Your opponent will have a tough shot to contend with . . . not a juicy set-up to pounce on for an almost certain winner.

NAIL THOSE HIGH VOLLEYS

One of the most frustrating experiences you can suffer on court is to foul up a high forehand volley that's just sitting there waiting to be belted.

The root of the problem usually is that, in your eagerness, you take too long a swing at the ball.

What you should do when a ball comes at you fairly high on your forehand side is to think of hitting it just the way you would hammer a nail above the level of your head.

You don't have that much time when you're up at the net. If you rear back and try to smash a high ball, it will probably be almost past you before you can get your racquet around to meet it.

What you've got to do is meet the ball out in front of you. You can see the ball better there, and hit it more firmly.

So when a high shot comes toward you at the net, just reach up with your racquet and hit the ball with the same motion you'd use if you were pounding a nail into a wall above the level of your head. Keep your wrist firm and punch the ball in the direction you want it to go. Nail it for a winner.

USE A
KARATE CHOP ON
BACKHAND VOLLEYS

One of the hardest shots to handle on the court is a high backhand volley up at the net.

If you just stick your racquet up to block the ball, the chances are good that you'll hit it long. What you have to do is chop, or slice the ball, so that it will come down inside your opponent's court.

An excellent way to develop this slicing action is to think of the high backhand volley as a kind of karate chop. That's the kind of motion you want on the stroke.

You should slash your racquet hand out and down, just as you would with a karate chop. Bring the bottom edge forward and down with a rapid slicing action as your racquet head approaches the ball.

If you do it correctly, this karate chop volley will produce a crisp shot that has some punch behind it and enough underspin to keep the ball in the court.

STICK THE BALL WITH AN ICE-PICK

It's important to hit volleys early. That permits you to meet the ball in front of you so you can send it back crisply and powerfully.

But a lot of players have trouble doing that for two reasons: they take too big a backswing and they hit the ball with too much wrist.

A good way to overcome the problem is to imagine that you have an ice pick sticking out from your racquet face. Then, when you volley from either the forehand or backhand side, pretend that you are sticking the ball with the ice-pick.

That will encourage you to let the racquet do the work for you on your volleys, rather than trying to help it too much by moving your hand and wrist.

So in hitting volleys, use a compact backswing, let your racquet do the work and imagine you're sticking the ball with an ice-pick.

DEFEND NET LIKE A GOALIE

When you advance to the net, it means you're on the offensive. You've assumed a commanding position on the court. But you've got to defend that position, of course . . . especially against passing shots.

If you have trouble doing that, keep in mind that your situation up there is similar in some ways to the situation of a hockey goalie, who also has to defend a net.

Think about how a goalie goes about his job. He crouches down with his stick out in front of him, poised to spring in any direction to block a flying puck. And depending on where the puck is, he shifts around to cut down the angle of attack by his opponents.

You should use the same principles to protect your position at the net on the tennis court. Crouch slightly with your racquet out in front of you and your weight forward, so that you're ready to pounce on any shot. And always adjust your position to reduce your opponent's angle of attack.

If you protect the net in tennis the way a goalie protects his net in hockey, you'll even achieve something that a goalie never does. You'll score some points.

5.
SPECIALTY
SHOTS

LEARN THE LOB

For many average players, learning to hit a lob seems to be one of those painful forms of self-improvement . . . like eating cabbage or reading uplifting books. They realize they'd be a lot better off if they did it. But they'd rather not. And as a result, they seldom do.

But most players would win a lot more often, especially in doubles, if they hit lobs a lot more often. That's because the lob can be an effective weapon in a number of ways.

For example, when you're behind your own baseline, you can lob over your opponent to drive him back from a commanding position at the net. In fact, the lob is the only way you can do that.

Or you can use the lob as an offensive weapon when you're up in front of your baseline and your opponent is at the net. A low lob over his outstretched racquet will move him back and may even win the point outright for you.

Using the lob, as some players apparently feel, doesn't stamp you as a sissy, or a beginner, or a bore. What it does is give you an immediate edge. So try it the next time you play a match. You'll find that lobbing is more fun than you think . . . especially because you'll win more games.

Wojtek Fibak

CUT UNDER LOBS

It's one thing to know, as many players do, that a smart play when an opponent's at the net is to lob the ball over his head. It's another thing, though, to get the ball high enough and deep enough so that he doesn't nail it for a winner.

Players who hit their lobs too short present opponents at net with an outright gift: a sitter that can be pounced on gleefully.

The problem when lobs go short usually is that a player tries to catch the ball flat on his racquet and lift it over his opponent's head with too much wrist action.

The key to hitting an effective lob is to cut under the ball with a firm wrist. So keep two things in mind.

First, think of meeting the bottom half of the ball and then bringing the racquet up and through it. This mental picture will help you hit the ball with the racquet face tilted slightly back, and give your shot the height you want.

The second thing to remember is to keep a firm wrist throughout the stroke. If your wrist isn't firm, you'll hit a weak floater, which can be picked off and smashed back by your opponent.

LOB THROUGH A GOALPOST

If you have trouble hitting lobs with real accuracy, there's a handy device that should help you a lot. That's to imagine there's a football goalpost across the net from you in the middle of the other court.

If you're like a lot of players, you have a problem getting the right height and depth on a lob. It will go long one time, and it will practically fall into the net man's lap the next.

The way to correct the problem is to try to hit your lobs over the crossbar of an imaginary goalpost, just the way a placekicker does with a football.

Don't go for distance. Just try to hit the ball hard enough, so that it will split the pretend uprights and land on the other side, inside the baseline.

That should help you to score some extra points, you might say.

GET UNDER THE BALL ON OVERHEADS

The overhead is one shot that seems to intimidate a lot of players. It's the stroke you have to hit when an opponent lifts a high lob at you. And one big reason it gives so many players so much trouble is that they don't know where to position themselves for the stroke.

But two-time Wimbledon champion Martina Navratilova says it's really quite simple. Get yourself right under the descending ball, she advises, so that if you were to let it fall without hitting it, then it would land on your nose or forehead.

To put yourself in that position, Navratilova adds, the first thing you should do when a lob comes your way is to keep your head up. Follow the ball all the way. A failure to do that, she says, accounts for most of the errors on overheads in club matches.

Then, to get the most power into the shot, Navratilova says you must station yourself so that you can meet the ball out in front of your body. Shuffle around under the ball until you're in that position. Or, as Navratilova says, until you've got the ball lined up so that if you were to let it fall without hitting it, it would drop right on your nose or forehead.

Martina Navratilova

CAST YOUR OVERHEADS

If the overhead gives you fits, then you may find it a bit easier if you remember that the proper motion for the stroke is similar to that used by a fisherman casting his line.

Keep that image in mind as you set up for the overhead, watching a lob drop toward you. That's what makes the overhead so tough. You've got to have the timing to meet a ball that's falling at you from above.

Copy the fisherman when you hit an overhead. Lean back as you cock your racquet to hit the ball. Then shift your weight forward, straighten your arm and snap your wrist sharply as you meet the ball. That's the motion you need to catch the ball right.

SMASH DOWN THE CENTER

Many players make one bad mistake when they attempt an overhead smash. They try to angle the shot away from the opponent rather than just concentrating on hitting the stroke well.

That's making a hard shot harder. What you should do on almost all overheads is aim the ball right down the middle of your opponent's court. There are a couple of reasons why.

First, it simplifies the shot. You don't have to worry about getting your feet into position for angling the overhead. Instead, you can concentrate on getting your racquet back and keeping your eyes on the ball.

Second, a smash down the middle is going to win the point for you in almost all cases, anyway. That's because the ball will have so much speed on it that it's likely to whiz past your opponent for an outright winner.

Don't make a hard shot harder by attempting to angle your overheads sharply away from your opponents. Settle for slamming the ball down the middle of your opponent's court.

SHOOT FOR THE MOONBALL

What can you do when you're facing an opponent who's blowing you off the court? One of the best counter-measures is a shot devised by Harold Solomon, who's one of the smallest, but shrewdest, tacticians in the pro game.

The shot Solomon has devised is known as the moonball. In effect, a moonball is a lob that's hit when both you and your opponent are playing back at the baseline. Instead of driving a conventional groundstroke at him, you loft a topspin shot that sails high over the net and lands just inside his baseline.

The key to hitting a moonball is to put topspin on it. And you do that by starting your swing with your racquet down below the level of your knees. Then, as you swing the racquet forward, bring it up sharply from low to high.

The moonball takes time and practice to perfect. But it's a great psychological weapon . . . as Solomon has proved . . . especially against that strapping opponent who always overpowers you. It will drive him crazy.

Harold Solomon

GET THE DROP ON YOUR OPPONENT

The drop shot is a great way to torment an opponent. The trouble is that many players only succeed in tormenting themselves with it because they mess it up so often. The reason is that they hit it wrong . . . and use it at the wrong times.

The shot must be made with a cupping motion that brings the racquet strings down and under the ball at contact.

The idea is to hit the ball so that it barely drops over the net and will bounce as many as three times before it reaches the middle of the other court. But too many players hit drop shots that land in that area to begin with. And that gives an opponent an easy set-up shot.

The only time the drop shot really works is when your opponent is at, or behind, his baseline . . . and you are in your own midcourt area ready to move to the net quickly to handle any return.

In that situation, you can force your opponent to rush in and make a scrambling return, which you should then be able to put away for an outright winner.

So remember: hit the drop shot shallow, and use it only when you're in midcourt and your opponent is deep in his court.

CATCH THE BALL FOR DROP SHOTS

Let's face it. The drop shot is not an easy stroke to master. It looks easy, but it isn't. It requires touch and finesse to hit properly.

A good way to develop this skill is to practice hitting the drop shot almost as though you are trying to catch the ball on your racquet. The idea is to tilt your racquet face back as it's about to meet the ball so that the strings of the racquet caress the back and bottom of the ball.

As you make contact, the racquet head should be moving on a downward and forward path, which will put some underspin on the ball. That helps you to control the ball, and prevents it from bouncing too far when it lands in your opponent's court.

Practice the drop shot as though you are trying to catch the ball on your racquet. The gentle caressing action of the strings around the back and bottom of the ball will produce a shot that falls short in your opponent's court . . . where it should.

SET A TRAP FOR DROP SHOTS

Chris Evert Lloyd is renowned for her deadly, steady groundstrokes. It is much less well known that she also possesses one of the most lethal drop shots in the game. And the way she combines the two skills is one of the things that makes her so tough to beat.

How does Chris do it? In effect, she sets a trap. She keeps her opponents pinned to the baseline with her flawless groundstrokes. And then when they hit a ball that brings her forward, she moves up and hits a drop shot.

The opponent then has to dash toward the net. And most of the time, only two things can happen . . . both of them bad for the opponent. Either she can't reach the ball. Or if she does, the return is a cripple that Chris can put away for a winner.

Use your own drop shot the way Chris Evert Lloyd does. Keep your opponents deep . . . and then surprise them with a ball that lands short.

6.
MATCH
WINNERS

GET IT BACK

Bjorn Borg once summed up his approach to the game this way: "I try to make the game as simple and uncomplicated as possible. I try to hit the ball over the net one more time than my opponent."

Borg's statement may seem obvious. But it's something that too often escapes many club players. They'll try to kill the ball, or to pull off a tough shot, in an attempt to win a point quickly. Much of the time all they'll succeed in doing is drive the ball long, or into the net, and lose the point.

But get the ball over the tennis net, and into the other court, and you're still in the point. That means using the best stroke at your disposal.

And that, of course, is the essence of what Borg was saying. Use your most reliable weapons in a tennis match. Keep the ball in play. And don't try to be fancy. If you succeed in getting the ball over the net one more time than your opponent on most points, there's no way you can lose.

Bjorn Borg

AIM DEEP DOWN THE MIDDLE

For most average players, the complexities of strategy aren't the important thing. Their main concern is simply getting the ball back over the net. Anything more is beyond them.

If it's beyond you, too, then tennis coach Vic Braden says there is one golden rule of strategy you should remember. And that rule is: always hit the ball deep down the middle of your opponent's court.

Imagine that there's a five-foot semicircle just in front of your opponent's baseline. Always aim for that, especially when you're playing at your own baseline.

That strategy can be trusted against any type of opponent. And it will help make you a winner, mainly because it gives you more room for error since the net is 6 inches lower in the middle than it is on the sides.

So aim your shots deep down the middle of the court to a five-foot semicircle in front of your opponent's baseline. It should help put you in the winner's circle.

KEEP YOUR SHOTS ON THE SIDEWALK

Do you tend to pull your forehands or backhands wide? If you do, it's likely that the problem probably lies in your follow-through.

Like many players who pull the ball wide, you probably view the tennis court as a gigantic expanse with plenty of room for a wrap-around follow-through.

But as tennis coach Vic Braden has noted, the court should actually be visualized as a long, narrow sidewalk. And with that in mind, you see how important it is to control your follow-through.

Take a moment sometime to stand in one corner of a court. If you first point your racquet down the sideline, and then crosscourt to the other corner, you'll have moved the direction of your follow-through only 19.1 degrees. And 19.1 degrees is all you have to play with.

Most players don't realize that. So when they see that one corner of the other court is open, they gleefully pounce on the ball, swing away . . . and send the ball 10 feet wide.

To avoid that, control your follow-through. Finish your stroke with the racquet pointing in the direction you want the ball to go.

Remember, a tennis court isn't a vast expanse. Think of it more as a long, narrow sidewalk.

Hana Mandlikova

HAVE A
HOME BASE

Too many players wander around the court during a match as if they were lost in a desert. They'll make a perfectly decent shot near one side of the court, watch the ball go over the net and then kind of meander around waiting for a return. When it comes back out of reach, they wonder what they did wrong.

What they did was commit a cardinal violation of a basic rule of tennis. And that is always to get back to the center of the court when you're rallying with an opponent from the baseline.

In fact, you should establish a kind of home base in the middle of the court, about two feet behind the baseline. From this spot, you're in a good position to move rapidly to the left or right to cover the court.

Then, once you've hit the ball, don't stand there admiring your shot or watching your opponent run after it. You're not out there as a spectator, remember.

Skip back immediately, to your home base . . . unless, of course, your opponent has hit a short ball that you have to run forward to retrieve. In that case, continue on up to the net.

Set up a home base about two feet behind the middle of the baseline. It will help you feel a lot more at home on the court.

PLAY EACH POINT A SHOT AT A TIME

Many players have an illusion about the game that's costing them dearly. They have a tendency to think that a lot of shots are exchanged on almost all the points they play in a match. They remember that really terrific rally a few years back when the ball crossed the net 25 times.

Actually, most points in club tennis are over pretty rapidly. They end after the serve, or the return of serve, or one or two shots after that.

So what's so bad about the illusion that a lot of shots are traded on most points?

The harm lies in the fact that players think they have more time to win a point than they really do. They'll think about setting up an opponent with a variety of shots. Or tell themselves that they may be playing miserably now, but they'll pull the point out on the eighth shot.

They don't have that luxury, of course. So the important thing to remember is to take good care of the shot you're hitting . . . because it's probably your last on that point.

If you can keep that in mind, and overcome the illusion that a lot of shots are exchanged on each point, you'll find that you'll concentrate better. And probably play better, too.

MOVE LIKE A BOXER

You can't hit a ball if you can't get to it. But too many players ignore that obvious fact. They keep shuffling around the court without any zeal, purpose or ambition. And then they wonder why so many balls elude them.

If you're going to get to as many balls as you can, the key is to move around the court the way a boxer moves around the ring. That is, in small skip steps.

As you pursue the ball, try to dance into position the way a boxer would. That way, you'll be balanced. And when you pull up to hit a stroke, you'll be able to plant yourself quickly and get your timing together for the shot. A ball hit while you're in balance is bound to be a sounder one.

Between points, also try to stay limber the way a boxer does between rounds. Jog in place a bit. That will help keep you loose and relaxed.

To hit better shots, move around the court the way a boxer moves around the ring. And score a few knockouts of your own.

KNOW THE CRUCIAL GAMES

Think about it. Tennis is one of the few sports in which you can score a victory without winning a majority of the points.

That's because if you're at your sharpest during the critical stages of a match, you can often beat another player who may outscore you slightly during other, less important stretches of play.

So it pays to know when those critical stages come. And as a rule they occur in the very first game . . . and in the seventh and eighth games . . . of a set.

The first game often sets the tempo for the entire match. So the worst thing you can do is start out too slowly, or con yourself into thinking that you can take your time about getting into the match. The curtain is up, so you've got to perform.

The seventh and eighth games are also critical because, from then on, one service break is usually decisive. Leading 4-3 or 5-3 with your own serve coming up, you can run out the set just by staying even. But your opponent can't win it without a long uphill fight.

Don't forget, you can be a winner in tennis without winning a majority of the points played . . . if you play at your best during the vital opening game and in the seventh and eighth games of any set.

John McEnroe

RETREAT FROM NO-MAN'S LAND

One place nobody wants to be in a match is caught in no-man's land . . . that midcourt area between the service line and the baseline. You're really vulnerable when a ball is hit at you there.

In those circumstances, what should you do? Try to volley the ball? Or retreat to the baseline and play the shot on the bounce?

For most players, hitting a volley from midcourt is a poor move. Even if you do reach it, you're not going to be able to hit any kind of solid shot.

Retreating to the baseline is better strategy for three reasons.

First, you have more time to get to the ball.

Second, you'll be able to set up properly and play the ball off the bounce . . . which should get you back in the point.

And third, you may be saving yourself a lot of trouble by letting the ball bounce. After all, it may be going out.

So don't go for the heroic volley when you're caught in no-man's land. Instead, be sensible. Hustle back to the baseline and play a deep groundstroke back to your opponent.

WATCH THE FEET

Wouldn't it be nice to know in advance where your opponent is going to hit the ball? Well, there is one tell-tale sign you can watch for that should help you. And that is to note how your opponent plants his feet before he hits the ball.

If he takes an open stance . . . that is, has his front foot off to the side and is more or less facing the net . . . it means he's likely to hit the ball on an angle crosscourt.

But if he takes a closed stance . . . that is, lines up more squarely to the ball . . . it means he'll probably hit it straight ahead, or down the line.

To be more specific, say you're facing a right-hander who's about to hit a forehand. If he takes an open stance, it means the ball will probably come to your right. A closed stance means to watch for a shot to your left.

Watch your opponent's stance to tell where the ball will probably be coming. And then, of course, watch the ball!

ANALYZE EASY MISTAKES

When you miss a shot in tennis that you thought was a piece of cake, the first thing you should do is try to figure out what went wrong.

To begin with, make sure that the shot really was a setup before you blame yourself. What may have appeared to be an easy chance may not have been that at all. Maybe you were off balance, for example, or maybe the angle wasn't there.

Don't look for excuses. But on the other hand, don't be hard on yourself if it wasn't really your fault.

Beyond that, there are some steps you can take if you do find you're missing a lot of easy shots.

First, make sure that your technique is correct . . . that you're remembering such basics as holding the racquet firmly and keeping your eyes on the ball.

Second, make a point of practicing those setups. Don't just casually tap them away in workouts. Play them for real.

And finally, if you do miss an easy shot, don't let it get you down. Just vow to do better next time.

Raul Ramirez

WHEN TO
GO FOR IT

It generally doesn't pay to try for spectacular winning shots. It's safer just to keep the ball in play and let your opponent make all of the mistakes.

However, there is a time when you should go for the winning shot. And that's when you are in a vulnerable position in a match.

Say that you've been pulled way off the court by a serve or approach shot . . . and that your opponent has moved up to the net to smother any routine return.

In this situation, it's actually good strategy to try for a winner with, for example, a tricky passing shot down the sideline.

Why go for a winner at this point? Because you know your opponent is in position to win the point easily if you don't. Then, too, it'll shake him up if you even come close to pulling off your shot. The next time in the same situation, he won't play with the same confidence.

So play percentage tennis most of the time by keeping the ball in play and forcing your opponent to make the mistakes. But, when you're in a really tight pinch, you're better off going for the winner . . . even though it's a tough shot to make.

WHEN TO EASE UP

There is one situation when it may well pay you not to play as hard as possible. That's when you're involved in a long, exhausting match that probably won't be decided until the very end.

The idea is to play all out on your own serve in order to make sure you win it. And then play all-out, as well, on the first two or three points of your opponent's serve.

Continue to push yourself on an opponent's serve only when the score gets to be 15-30 or better in your favor . . . or 30-all. In other words, when you have a real chance to break his serve.

But when your opponent gets ahead by 30-15 or better on his serve, relax. Deliberately hit your next shot short or lob, or go for a winner, in order to shorten the rally.

If you let up this way, your opponent will expend about one-third more energy attempting to break your serve than you do trying to break his. And when the match gets down to those vital final games, you'll be fresher and in a stronger position.

So ease up when your opponent gets ahead on his serve in a close tennis match. Some of the world's top players say that's the way they've pulled out many a narrow victory.

Bob Lutz

PULLING OUT OF A SLUMP

You don't have to be a pro to fall into a slump. All players are subject to slumps. And generally speaking, there are two major reasons for them.

One is using a playing style that doesn't suit you. You might be copying a style of play that you happen to admire, but can't really execute.

If you don't have solid groundstrokes, for instance, you probably should be trying to end points quickly rather than extending the rallies. Or if you can hit volleys and cover the court well, you should be moving up to the net at every opportunity . . . not hanging back at the baseline.

The second big reason for slumps is a decline in physical condition. When you're not as fit as you should be, nothing . . . neither technique nor tactics . . . is going to help you against a tough opponent.

So the next time you lose a string of matches you think you should have won, try to figure out why you're in the slump before you get depressed about it. The chances are that you've either adopted a playing style that's wrong for you or you're not in the kind of shape you should be.

SLOW THE PACE WHEN YOU'RE BEHIND

Many players panic or get discouraged when an opponent breaks serve and goes ahead early in a match.

But they shouldn't because there's a good device for getting out of this predicament. That's to slow down the pace of play and let the pressure of being slightly ahead wear down your opponent mentally.

Two things happen to your opponent when you proceed as slowly as possible, without actually stalling, between points and games.

First, he becomes uncomfortable not playing at his own pace. Hanging on to a service break for an entire set is a hard job. And most players with slim leads want to play quickly. Slow them down and you'll disrupt their games.

Second, your opponent has more time to think about the slim lead, and about what can go wrong, when you slow things down. And that can cause him to become impatient or indecisive, forcing more mistakes.

Don't change your basic game just because an opponent breaks your serve early in a set. Instead, slow down the pace of play to disrupt his game and to get yourself back in the match.

BEAR DOWN WHEN YOU'RE AHEAD

Some players have trouble holding onto a lead . . . especially when they're ahead of an opponent they're not supposed to beat. They think: "Hey, what am I doing beating this guy?"

To keep the lead and close out a match, it's vital, first, not to ease up, not to feel sorry for your opponent. A lead has a way of evaporating if you relax.

So continue doing what you have been doing. If you've been winning by playing aggressive tennis, for instance, keep it up. Keep up the pressure.

Don't get conservative, hoping you can close out the match before your opponent wakes up. That's not the way you took the lead to begin with, and that's not the way you're going to keep it.

Just concentrate on one shot at a time when you're ahead. And avoid relishing your victory in advance. It can be fatal, for example, to tell yourself, "Now if I can just hold on to this game, I've got him."

Simply think about the next point. And remember that if you win two out of three points, you'll never lose a match in your life.

CHART YOUR WAY TO BETTER PLAY

Like most players, you probably think you have a good idea of what your strengths and weaknesses are. But do you really?

There's one way to find out for sure . . . and to increase your chances of winning at the same time. And that's by charting your matches.

How do you chart a match? First, of course, you've got to line up a friend or relative to do the actual charting while you're playing. You can offer to chart his matches if he'll chart yours.

The charting system you use can be as sophisticated or as simple as you like. You can get one of the commercial charting sheets that have been introduced in recent years. They're like the ones used in baseball and basketball. And they'll permit you to keep a complex record of a match; they'll even tell you things like the angle of a shot.

Or you can use your own charting system and gear it to your own needs. It can be as basic as a record of first serves in, double faults, and winners and errors on each stroke.

At the end of the match, you can count them up and get a good idea of where you did well . . . and where you didn't. In other words, what your strengths and weaknesses really are.

7.
STRATEGY
POINTERS

PLAY THE PERCENTAGES

One of the oldest, and truest, axioms in tennis is that most matches are won by the player who makes fewer errors . . . not the one who hits more winners.

That's something to be remembered by every club player, just as it is by the pros at Wimbledon or the U.S. Open.

When you're in a tournament match, the key is to play it safe and steady. Your opponent, don't forget, is just as nervous as you are. Let him or her make the mistakes. Don't go for a big shot . . . in the beginning, at least. Play as steadily as you can.

Place your first serves as deep in the service box as possible. When you return serve, concentrate simply on getting the ball back over the net. And probe for an opponent's weakness. If you discover it's the backhand, hit mostly to that side.

Tell yourself that no matter what, you're not going to be the one to make the errors. If you have to, just bloop the ball over the net until you hit your stride.

And remind yourself that most matches, at any level, are won by the player who makes fewer errors . . . not by the one who hits more winners.

Adriano Panatta

FIND THE WEAKNESS

If you want to get an instant reading on an opponent you're facing for the first time, use these three tests during the warm-up or the first few points.

The first test is deliberately to hit an easy, short ball to the opponent's forehand side . . . and then to his backhand side. If he flubs the shot on one side, you know there is some weakness there.

The second test is to gauge how steady your opponent is. Hit a series of shots to approximately the same spot and see how long your opponent can keep getting the ball back. If he gets impatient, you know there is weakness there.

The third test is simply to hit a series of shots to the corners and to observe whether your opponent moves better to his left or to his right. Once you know which direction gives him the most trouble, you have found still another weakness.

Use these three tests to analyze an opponent quickly. You'll probably detect a weakness you can use to win.

ATTACK
THE BACKHAND

To be a constant winner, there is one place where you should try to attack your opponent: on the backhand.

It's true that some players have better backhands than forehands. But research at the Vic Braden Tennis College in California shows that you'll generally win if you go for the other player's backhand.

That's partly because most players don't have that much confidence in their backhands. So they're half-way psyched out even before they hit the ball.

But even if they can hit backhands, they can't do as much with the ball as they can with forehands.

For one thing, they have to set up a good deal faster to hit a backhand. That's because they have to meet the ball farther out in front of the body than they do on a forehand. So if they're the slightest bit late . . . and they will be some of the time, they'll mis-hit it or barely get it back.

But most importantly, your opponent . . . even if he has a fairly good backhand . . . will almost always hit a shot that's higher and softer than his forehand. The reason is that most players hit backhands with underspin, so they loft you a ball that you can do a lot more with on the return.

TAKE A TIP
FROM TILDEN

It's often been said that Bill Tilden, who was perhaps the greatest player who ever picked up a racquet, never played the same match twice.

That is, he adapted his game to meet the challenge at hand. He never kidded himself. He sized up his opponent's game, and his own, during each match. And then he adjusted his style and strategy accordingly.

Basically, there are three ways you can use that kind of instant analysis to improve your game.

First, learn to study your opponent as he is actually playing . . . and not with preconceived notions of how you expect him to play. Observe his strengths and his weaknesses carefully and plan your strategy around them.

Second, study yourself. Suppose your big weapon is usually your serve, but for some reason it goes sour on you. Don't just shake your head. Try to figure out what's wrong.

And finally, study the match as it goes along. Is your opponent, say, nailing your cross-court forehands for consistent winners? Obviously, you should try something different.

Every match is a brand new test. So treat it that way by analyzing your opponent, yourself and the flow of the match as it goes along . . . the way Bill Tilden did.

RETURN SPIN
WITH SPIN

When you face a pretty good player, you can expect to see lots of balls with spin coming at you. Returning a spinning ball calls for a special technique. It isn't as easy as returning an ordinary flat ball.

Basically, there are two kinds of spin that can be put on a tennis ball. There's topspin, which sends the ball rotating toward the receiver. And there's underspin, which rotates away from the receiver.

The key is to return spin with spin. So watch how your opponent hits the ball. If he brings his racquet up to meet it, expect topspin. And prepare to return it with topspin of your own by taking your racquet from low to high . . . coming up to meet the ball squarely.

What you'll be doing is counteracting your opponent's spin and feeding him some of his own medicine.

On the other hand, if your opponent's racquet goes down from high to low, expect underspin. And react accordingly.

If you ignore the spin, the chances are that you'll pop a topspin ball in the air . . . and hit an underspin ball into the net.

The way to handle spin, quite simply, is to retaliate with the same kind of spin yourself.

Eddie Dibbs

MOVE YOUR OPPONENT AROUND

It is possible to stay in the backcourt and still play aggressively . . . as champions like Eddie Dibbs have proved.

The secret lies in knowing how to move your opponent around until you force an error, or get a short ball, that you can hit into an open corner for a winner.

What you're trying to do from the backcourt is to keep your opponent off-balance by hitting the ball deep to one side, and then deep to the other.

To do that, of course, you've got to have reliable groundstrokes. And patience, too. You've got to be content to hit from side to side with authority, waiting for an error or a short ball. Above all, you don't want to hit floaters that will sit up begging to be clobbered.

Depending upon where you have maneuvered your opponent, you can hit cross-court or straight ahead. The safer shot is cross-court because you have more area to hit into and also a greater margin for error in clearing the net.

You can be aggressive, and a winner, from the backcourt. The secret lies in learning how to move your opponent around the court.

ATTACK ON HARD COURT

What's the secret to success when you're playing on a hard court like those made of asphalt or cement?

The ball bounces low and fast on a hard court. And the slick surface means that an attacking game is what will usually win for you. So you've got to get to the net as soon as you can.

Once you're up there, you'll have the upper hand. Your opponent won't have much time to get to the ball and try to blast it past you because of the low, fast bounce.

What you should try to do, as a result, is play a serve-and-volley game. That is, try to get something on your serve and then to rush the net where you can put the ball away with a volley.

When you're receiving serve on a hard court, shorten your backswing. That'll help you to cope with the low, skidding bounces . . . and to attack the ball so the server will have trouble getting to the net.

In short, get aggressive on hard courts.

BE PATIENT ON SLOW COURTS

What makes slow courts, like clay and Har-Tru, so slow? It's because the surface is coarse. The ball bites into it, slows down and then bounces higher than it does on other surfaces.

How do you win on slow courts? It can be summed up in one word: patience.

The high, slow bounce gives you time to chase down your opponent's shot, set up and take a good swing at it. Of course, the slow conditions do the same thing for him.

That means your chances of hitting a winning shot on a slow court are less than they are on a fast one. Your opponent will be able to run down more balls.

So on a slow court, you've got to be prepared to engage in long rallies from the baseline. Aim to hit the ball deep down the middle. If you do . . . and if you're patient . . . there's not much that your opponent can do, except to hope that you miss before he does.

Even if you're an attacking type player, you've got to resist that urge just to rush up to the net. Your opponent will have plenty of time to set up and easily blow the ball by you.

So be patient. Wait for a short ball or a floater that you can pounce on with a shot that will put your opponent on the defensive.

AVERT THE UPSET

It's not a nice feeling, but it happens to every player at one time or another. For some reason, you're losing to a player who you figured to beat easily.

What can you do to pull out the match? They say you should always change a losing game. But in this case, that's probably not necessary . . . at least if you have the superior game.

What you should try to do is get the other player to think more . . . think about the situation and think about how he's going to hold onto the lead. In other words, make him put a little pressure on himself.

And how do you do that?

One way is to increase the time that the ball is in the air by slowing down your shots and maybe even looping some of them back. That will increase his anxiety level, especially if he has a short fuse, by forcing him to think longer about his next shot.

Another way is to throw a few surprises at him. Rush the net once or twice, for example, even if that's not your normal style. It may bother him, and it will certainly give him something to think about.

When you're losing a match that you should be winning, simply think about getting the other guy to think.

Victor Pecci

BREAK THROUGH ON BREAK POINT

One of the toughest points to play in a match is break point. When you're the receiver, it's your big chance. And how you handle it can make a big difference in the outcome of the match.

What should you do? The main thing is to have a plan. Before the server begins his delivery, decide where you're going to hit your return. And as best as you can, work out a general plan for the point.

What should that plan be? Above all, it should allow you to take advantage of your strengths and to cash in on your opponent's weaknesses. If the cross-court forehand is your big shot, for example, try to set things up so you can use it.

And try to attack the server's weak spots. He must have some . . . or else you wouldn't be on the verge of breaking his serve. Remember the mistakes he made, and try to let him make them again.

You've got to break your opponent's serve at least once to win a set. So when you get to break point, don't throw a precious opportunity away. Have a plan.

LOB OR PASSING SHOT?

Your opponent is up at the net and he or she hits you a ball back around your own baseline. What should you do? Lob over his head? Or try to drive a passing shot out of his reach down the sideline?

A good rule to keep in mind when you have to make that choice is this one: use the lob when you're behind your baseline, and try a passing shot when you're in front of the baseline.

The lob is the better option when you're behind your baseline because your opponent will probably have time to get to the ball if you attempt a passing shot.

But when you're in front of your baseline and your opponent's at the net, then you should definitely try a passing shot. You're close enough to him so that he'll have little time to react and to reach the ball as it streaks past him on one side or the other.

When your opponent is at the net, remember to use a lob if you're in back of your baseline, and a passing shot down the sideline if you're in front of your baseline.

Rod Laver

LEARN FROM THE DINKER

Probably the most irritating character you can play is the dinker. He's the guy who always plays it safe, never takes any chances and rarely seems to have much fun.

Dinkers may drive their opponents crazy, but there's a lesson in their maddening tactics for all players. And that is to remember that you win far more points on your opponent's errors than you do on your own winners.

Too many players, especially men, have visions of blowing their opponents off the court. But tennis doesn't work that way . . . even at the top.

None of the great stars of the game, Bjorn Borg or Chris Evert Lloyd or Rod Laver, can remember a single match they won by cracking off winner after winner. All they can remember is their opponents' errors.

So reconcile yourself to the fact that the day will never come when you overwhelm an opponent by hitting with wild abandon and unbelievable accuracy. Remember the dinker, who lets his opponents beat themselves. Sure, nobody loves him. But you can bet that his shelves are lined with trophies.

BLUNT THE BIG HITTER

Many players make the mistake of trying to out-gun the big hitters they meet on court. There are two things wrong with that approach.

By hitting the tennis ball back to your opponent at a fast pace, you are giving him the kind of ball he likes. And by playing at your opponent's pace, rather than at your own, you disrupt your own natural rhythm.

The best thing to do against the big hitter is simply to take that speed away by hitting chips and slices all through the match.

Balls hit that way slow up as they cross the net. If your opponent wants to return those shots with any speed, he's going to have to generate his own power. And that can lead to errors on his part.

It's a mistake to try to out-hit the big hitter in tennis. Instead, give him a variety of underspin shots . . . and watch him start to make the mistakes.

CROSS UP
THE BASELINER

One of the most frustrating experiences you can have on court is to face a steady, relentless baseliner . . . a player who won't budge from the backcourt. Is there anything you can do to overcome the baseliner?

Yes, there are three things.

First, and most importantly, don't give in to your frustration by playing impulsively and impatiently. If you do, you'll lose control of the match. Instead, learn to be as patient as he or she is.

Second, vary your shots more than usual in an effort to break the rhythm of the point. Most backcourt players come up to the net only when they want to. So try to make them come in when you want them to. A good way to do it is to hit a deep ball and then a short angled one . . . or to send over a drop shot.

Finally, come up to the net as soon as you can because that will unsettle the baseliner. But beware of rushing in too fast, since he is likely to have a wide range of lobs and passing shots.

BEWARE OF CHANGING YOUR GAME

One of the most popular axioms in tennis is that you should always change a losing game. But should you?

That depends on whether or not you're really playing a losing game.

Too often, players will change an otherwise sound style of play because an opponent has made a couple of good or lucky shots. And changing can be disastrous if you happen to change to a style that you're not really equipped to play.

The best thing to do when you are losing a match is to take a moment between games to analyze calmly both your game and your opponent's. Don't rush into changing anything.

If you are beating yourself with errors, then you should remind yourself of tennis fundamentals . . . and concentrate on watching the ball better.

If you are being beaten by a lot of strong winning shots, review your strategy. Maybe you've worked yourself into a predictable pattern of play, making it easy for the opponent to anticipate your shots. So try varying the pace of play.

Don't change a losing game just for the sake of changing. You may just lose even faster that way. Stick to your basic style. But try to cut down your errors. And vary the pace of play.

HIT WIDE BALLS CROSSCOURT

When an opponent sends you scrambling wide to chase down a shot, you should almost always do one thing: hit the ball back crosscourt.

The general tendency is to take the other option and hit the ball pretty much straight ahead . . . or down-the-line.

But it's safer and wiser to go crosscourt on wide shots, for three reasons.

First, you'll be hitting over the middle of the net. And it's six inches lower there than it is at the sideline where a down-the-line shot would go. So you're less apt to hit a crosscourt shot into the net.

Second, you have more court to hit into by aiming the ball crosscourt. A tennis court measures 82½ feet diagonally and 78 feet down the line. That means you have as much as an extra 4½ feet to play with on your shot.

And third, by hitting crosscourt you put your opponent in the same position you were. He has to decide whether to go crosscourt or down-the-line on his return. And he may be tempted to thread the needle by going down-the-line.

So play the percentages on wide shots. Go crosscourt.

8.
MENTAL
REMINDERS

Billie Jean King

MAKE EVERY POINT MATTER

Concentration is as vital to success in tennis as it is in any other sport. But how do you achieve it?

Rod Laver and Billie Jean King, two of the greatest champions of our time, each have little devices that help them concentrate on court . . . and that might help you.

Laver says that you've got to wipe everything out of your mind except the ball. Never mind your opponent, or the weather, or the blonde on the next court. Make that ball an obsession. If you can get yourself into that kind of a trance, it will be hard for anything else to disturb your thoughts.

Billie Jean King's way of concentrating is to play every single point as if it were the decisive one in a game. That way, she says, she focuses on one point at a time, knowing that collectively they will add up to the match.

Try Laver's method of making an obsession of following the ball, or King's of pretending that every point is a decisive one. It may not win you the titles they won at Wimbledon. But it should win you some points you might otherwise have lost.

MASTER YOUR NERVES

Why do players get nervous before a match? After all, it isn't a bullfight where you might get gored, or a boxing match where you might get your bell rung.

The reason any real competitor gets nervous before an important match is because it's a test . . . a mental test. And that's where you're most vulnerable on the court.

If you lose because the other player is stronger or faster or just better, that's a fact of life. And you can't do much about it.

But if you flunk the mental test . . . if you collapse on the big points . . . then your self-image takes a beating. It's no disgrace, for example, to be outrun by your pet beagle. But to be outsmarted by him? That's something else.

So how can you build yourself up mentally to withstand the pressures of an important match?

One suggestion from Dr. Allen Fox, a psychologist and top college coach, is to play matches which mean something fairly often. Enter club or local tennis tournaments. Or play other matches for something like a round of beers to increase the pressure a bit.

In other words, it takes practice to master your nerves in tennis . . . just as it does to master your strokes.

APPLY THE PRESSURE

It's usually assumed that the winner of a match is the player who hit the most aces, or was steadier from the baseline, or knocked off the most volleys. You'll hear that John beat Bill, but rarely that John made Bill lose.

Yet that is what usually happens. Most of the time, the player who wins does it by forcing the other player to lose.

How does he do that? He does it by putting pressure on the opponent at the right times . . . by seeing to it that the opponent can't play his best game.

For example, say that your opponent has been hitting terrific groundstrokes from his baseline all afternoon. Then, on a crucial point, you send him a deep ball and suddenly run up to the net behind it. That puts new and unexpected pressure on your opponent. And he's likely to respond to it by fluffing his return.

Similar situations come up all the time in a match. The trick is to be alert to them, and then take advantage of them.

Pressure can be your ally, or your enemy, on court. Make it your ally and you'll find that you don't have to hit the most aces, or outstroke an opponent, in order to win.

ACKNOWLEDGE TENSION

What can you do when you're ahead in a match and then, suddenly, your game falls apart? Gardner Mulloy, who's won 52 U.S. titles, more than any man in history, has some suggestions.

First, says Mulloy, switch your racquet to your other hand between points. When your game starts deteriorating, your natural tendency is to start gripping the racquet tighter and tighter. Switching hands gives you a chance to relax.

Second, deliberately hit the next ball into the fence. The reason you're doing so poorly is probably because most of your shots have been landing in the net. By hitting the ball long, you'll force yourself to recognize the problem and get back to hitting the ball the way you should.

And on the changeover, Mulloy says, pour some water on the insides of your wrists . . . especially on your hitting arm. And do it slowly. That should help cool you down and relax you.

But the real secret to staying ahead in a match, Mulloy adds, is to keep pressing when you're in the lead. Hit out, he says. Remember the basics . . . and never let up.

STAY FOOTLOOSE IN TIGHT SPOTS

One of the realities of tennis, like any other sport, is that a player is going to get tense and nervous during an important match.

It's a natural reaction, of course, to pressure. But what can be done to overcome this tension . . . to reduce the impact it has on your game?

The first thing to do is to recognize that fear inhibits movement . . . on your strokes, on your footwork, on everything.

A good cure for tennis nerves is the one devised by Arthur Ashe. The great champion used to write himself a note that said: "Keep your feet moving." He'd leave it beside his chair on the sidelines as a reminder at every changeover.

Ashe realized that, under pressure, the first thing that goes is the feet. A severe attack of nerves can all but immobilize them. And a player who's feeling the pressure will stand there frozen on the baseline . . . unable to get a quick jump on a ball he could ordinarily reach.

So to cope with tension during a big match, tell yourself to keep your feet moving.

GO AHEAD, BE SUPERSTITIOUS

Tennis is a game of repetition and routine and, above all, pressure on the player. So it is not suprising that many players, even the pros, develop little superstitions. Not because they believe in mumbo-jumbo, but because it helps them live more comfortably with the pressure.

The pros like to recreate the conditions of victory, hoping that if they repeat a routine they used before a previous win, it will help them produce another win. Thus, many pros, like Dick Stockton, continue to wash out and wear the same outfit if they've had success in it.

Other tennis stars have other superstitions. For example, Jimmy Connors always bounces the ball in multiples of four before he serves. Chris Evert Lloyd rotates her wrist while she waits for her opponent to serve. Vitas Gerulaitis carefully walks around the outside of the court when changing sides.

Those are some of the superstitions of the stars. They may not help. But the players think they do, which helps make them feel more comfortable on court. And that's what counts at any level of the game.

Dick Stockton

IGNORE THE PSYCH

Psyching is one of the oldest ploys known to tennis. The object is to make an opponent think. It's not important what he thinks about . . . just so long as he starts to take his mind off the match.

Then, his concentration is disrupted. His strokes become spotty. And his tennis game comes unglued.

The classic psych artist is the guy who says something to his opponent like: "I don't care what everyone says about your serve. I think it's great."

Now, the opponent knows it's a joke. But isn't there always a grain of truth in humor? So he starts to think about his serve. And before you know it, he can't get one in to save his life.

How do you deal with the psych in tennis?

Basically, you should remember that a psych will work only if you let it. If you have confidence in your game and the discipline to ignore a psych, it can't affect you.

But if you have a bit of the devil in you yourself, you can always give the guy who tries to psych you on your serve a taste of his own medicine. You can reply: "Hey, I just wish I had a serve like yours. You're the closest thing to Roscoe Tanner in this county."

That'll give him something to think about.

STAY COOL AGAINST THE SUPERIOR PLAYER

One of the basic truths of the game is that no matter how good you are, there's somebody better. And you always seem to be scheduled to play him next week!

What can you do to avoid public disgrace . . . maybe not to win, but at least to lose with self-respect?

Basically, you should just try to stay cool. Suspend all your expectations of being humiliated, on the one hand, or of pulling off a big upset, on the other.

Too many players become awed when they face superior opponents. They get so tense that they can barely swing their racquets. Or they race around, out of control, trying to over-compensate for their inadequate strokes.

The best thing to do is simply not think about the situation at all and to play your normal game as best you can.

Go with your best shots and hope they keep you in the match. There's no point in trying leaping backhand overheads, for example, if you rarely hit them. You'll just go down the tubes that much faster.

Finally, if you lose, don't alibi or apologize to your opponent for failing to give him a better match.

No apologies are necessary. He's been on the other side of the net in his time, too, remember.

WORK ON YOUR CONCENTRATION

Most players find they can concentrate really well for a few games, or for a set or two, at most.

Bjorn Borg, though, has the ability to maintain really intense concentration through an entire match . . . no matter how long it is. And that unique ability is one of the things that sets Borg apart from all other tennis players.

How does Borg do it?

He does it by practicing his concentration just as hard as his strokes. When Borg goes out to practice, he doesn't joke or clown around like many players, even some pros. He's all business, all the time.

Borg plays practice sets just as though they were real sets. He doesn't relax and allow any lapses in his concentration.

Borg doesn't suggest that the average player can do the same thing . . . right away, anyway. The ability to concentrate is something that has to be built up over a period of time, like endurance in running.

But if you work at it, if you practice your concentration as well as your strokes, you'll find that it will work for you a whole lot better during a match.

MAKE ONLY POSITIVE MISTAKES

When you blow an easy shot, do you blow your stack? Do you throw the kind of tantrum that might get you committed if it were happening anywhere except on a tennis court?

If you do, a good way to keep your emotions in check, and to help your game at the same time, is to make only positive mistakes. A positive mistake is something that you learn from, rather than a negative mistake that you brood about.

Look at it this way. After you make a bad error on the court, you can react in one of two ways. You can either get upset and bad-mouth yourself. Or you can take the positive approach.

You can determine what you did wrong and tell yourself that you'll hit the shot better if you don't make the same mistake again. That is, you reinforce positively the correct approach to the stroke.

Maybe you failed to get your racquet back, or didn't watch the ball, or didn't follow through. Whatever the problem, learn from your errors. Don't suffer from them. Recognize them for what they are: errors, an important part in the learning process.

Obviously, you're going to get a lot farther in tennis, and enjoy it a lot more, if you react that way to your mistakes. So make sure that your errors are positive, and not negative, ones.

9.
DOUBLES
LESSONS

Anne Smith & Kathy Jordan

PICK THE RIGHT PARTNER

Picking a regular doubles partner isn't always easy. Some players just aren't suited for doubles. Can you imagine General George Patton making a good doubles partner, for example? Or Archie Bunker?

The keys to finding the right partner are to locate someone with whom you're compatible and whose playing style complements yours.

You want a compatible person because it will obviously be more fun playing tennis with someone you like. And that way, your partnership is more likely to survive those awkward moments when one of you blows an easy shot.

Your team will be more successful, too, if your partner's playing style complements yours. If you're a steady type player, for example, look for a more fiery partner who can put the ball away . . . even though he may make his share of errors in trying to do it.

Finally, try to find someone who knows there's a time to poach and a time not to poach, a time to shout and a time to shut up, a time to yell "mine" and a time to yell "yours."

LEAD WITH YOUR STRENGTH

It's surprising how few doubles players give any thought to who should serve first. If one partner is closer to the baseline when a match is to begin, the other one will often say: "Okay, you serve."

But that can be a big mistake in a close match. Because the decision on who serves first can make the difference between winning and losing.

The rule is that a team should always have the better server go first in each set.

For one thing, it means that he or she will serve twice in the first six games of the set, while the weaker server will serve only once. And for another, it means that you're unlikely to fall very far behind.

Consider what would happen if you start with your weaker server and the other team starts with its better one. Assuming that the better servers on each team hold their serves, and the weaker ones lose theirs, your team will drop the set 6-4.

So lead with your strength. Have your better server go first.

GET THAT FIRST SERVE IN

Should you serve in doubles the same way that you serve in singles? Definitely not . . . because doubles puts different demands on a server.

For one thing, you've got to try to get your first serve in every time. In singles, you can afford to take more chances on a hard first serve because a deep second delivery will generally still keep your opponent from taking control of the point.

But in doubles, the receiver can pounce on a second serve and drill the ball through your partner at the net for an easy winner.

Beyond that, you should try to place most of your serves to the receiver's weaker side, usually the backhand. Otherwise, as in the case of the weak second serve, the receiver may be able to use his or her better stroke to go on the attack.

Finally, you always move up to the net after your serve. Most points in doubles are won at the net. So you've got to get up there.

Don't serve in doubles the same way you do in singles. Always get your first serve in. Place it to the receiver's weaker side. And move up to the net immediately.

PLAY WITH CARE ON THE BASELINE

In doubles, most points are won by the team that gets control of the net. But what can you do when you're on the other side? When you and your partner are in the backcourt and your opponents have command of the net?

Don't worry. All is not lost . . . if you follow two basic strategies.

The first is that if you have to hit a ball from behind your baseline, always lob it. When you're that deep in your court, a normal groundstroke will take so long to reach the net that your aged aunt would have time to stick her racquet out and dink back a winner.

But when you're in front of your baseline, the best move is usually a soft shot aimed down the middle of the court between your opponents. At the club level, most partners play too far apart. So a ball that's sent between them can be tough for them to cover.

But what if they catch on after a while and begin to move closer together? In that case, simply start aiming your shots toward the sideline.

Veteran partners Bob Hewitt & Frew McMillan (back-
ground) defend from baseline against an aggressive pair.

PRETEND YOU HAVE A 12-FOOT ROPE

Success in doubles depends a lot, of course, on team-work. And a big part of that involves covering the court as efficiently as possible.

One of the best ways to do that is to imagine that you and your partner are linked together by a 12-foot rope.

You'll quickly see why, if you watch any of the top pro doubles teams in action. The two players seldom get too close to each other . . . or too far apart. If they did either, they would open up too much of the tennis court for their opponents to aim at, either down the sidelines or up the middle. They are, in effect, tied together by an imaginary 12-foot rope.

And you should be, too, in your doubles matches. Keep track of your own and your partner's movements so that you neither break that rope nor let it droop to the ground.

And when you lose a point, check the imaginary rope if the other team scored a clean winner. The chances are that the rope either broke as the tennis ball went right between the pair of you, or that you let the rope trail on the ground as the ball sped out of reach down the sideline.

AIM AT THE HIP

Here's a situation that comes up fairly often in doubles. You're in the forecourt engaged in a hot exchange with an opponent who's just across the net. Where should you hit the ball?

There's one place almost guaranteed to win you the point. That's a ball aimed at the player across the net right between his hip and his armpit on his racquet side.

It's really difficult to return a shot that's drilled to the racquet side from close quarters . . . as you know if you've ever tried it.

The best you can do, if you can do anything at all, is defend yourself by bringing the racquet up and trying to block the ball with a backhand volley. You can't get anything on it. And even if the ball does go over the net, you're immediately on the defensive again.

Play it smart when you're involved in an exchange up at the net in doubles. Aim the ball between the hip and the armpit on the racquet side of the opponent across the net.

DON'T APOLOGIZE

You hear it all the time in doubles. One player will make a mistake and almost instantly say something like: "Sorry, partner, I blew it."

An apology seems to be an obvious and natural reaction in the circumstances. But Dr. Allen Fox, who's both a tennis coach and a psychologist, says that you shouldn't do it. You should keep your lips closed and get on with the game . . . for three reasons.

First, an apology only emphasizes the mistake. You're much better off putting it straight out of your mind and concentrating on the next point.

Second, an apology can give your opponents across the net a psychological boost. Hearing you worry and talk about your errors can only help their confidence.

Third, your partner is likely to get more upset with you if you apologize. Talking about your mistakes only underlines them in his or her mind. And if you do it enough, it may seem that you're making more errors than you really are.

So suppress that urge to apologize. Don't look for forgiveness. Look to the next point.

10.
PRACTICE
POINTERS

PUT FUN IN YOUR PRACTICE

Like most people, you probably play the game for fun. And there's not much fun in the usual practice session.

There can be, though, if you inject some of the fun of real competition in your practice drills. That way, you'll enjoy working out with a practice partner and do it more often, which can only improve your game for actual matches.

For example, practice adding depth to your ground-strokes by rallying with your partner from the baseline. And add competitive interest by awarding points. You can agree, say, that the first player to hit a ball inside the service line loses the point.

Or practice hitting to opposite corners of the court. You can go either crosscourt, backhand to backhand, or trade shots from the other corners, forehand to forehand. The player who hits the ball short, or in the center of the court, loses the point.

If you make a game out of your practice sessions, they'll not only be more fun, they'll help you get more fun out of your actual game.

Evonne Goolagong

USE THE PERFECT PRACTICE PARTNER

Would you like a practice partner who's always available, always returns the ball and never criticizes a poor shot? Who wouldn't?

That ideal is as near as the backboard at your club or any large flat wall in your neighborhood. And you ought to use it as often as you can to improve, and to groove, your strokes.

The best way to use a backboard, or a wall, to practice your strokes is first to stand well back.

Remember: the net is 39 feet away from the baseline on a tennis court. By standing well back from the backboard, the ball will come back to you so that you can hit it after only one bounce . . . just as you would in an actual match.

Practice hitting forehands and backhands in succession, first one and then the other. Angle some of your shots so that you have to run to reach the ball on the next rebound.

And don't get sloppy. Use your best form on each shot. Watch the ball. Get your racquet back early. And follow through properly. Otherwise, you'll just develop poor habits at the backboard that will yield poor results on the court.

TRY NEW SCORING METHODS

Do you have a weakness in your game you know you should work on? But do you put it off because you want to play, not practice?

There is a way you can have it both ways . . . work on that weakness and still have the fun of playing a match. That's by changing the way you keep score so that a big emphasis is placed on your weakness and you're rewarded when you overcome it.

For example, suppose you're so afraid of double-faulting that you never hit any serve really hard, you always float your second serve across the net as timidly as you can.

Why not try this variation in the rules for a while with your opponent? Give the server three serves on each point. And if he scores an ace on the third serve, he wins not just the point . . . but the game, too.

Or say that you don't rush up to the net nearly as often as you know you should. A way to overcome that hang-up is to agree with your opponent that a player will lose the game . . . and not just the point . . . if he misses any shot back at the baseline, except the return of serve. That should be enough of an incentive to force you off of the baseline and up to the net.

There are, obviously, any number of scoring variations that can be devised. So why not use one of these, or invent one of your own, if you have a weakness that needs work?

Roscoe Tanner

PUT MORE SERVES ON TARGET

Roscoe Tanner has the quickest and most feared serve in professional tennis today. We've timed it, using the TENNIS magazine radar gun, at a blistering 130 miles an hour.

But all that power would be useless, of course, if Tanner couldn't also get the ball in consistently.

Tanner has a practice ritual that helps him keep his big serve in control . . . and that could help your serve, too. Tanner suggests that you take a basket of balls out on a practice court and set up targets in each corner of both service courts. Make the targets fairly large at first. About the size of your warm-up jacket or pants.

Then, hit 10 or 20 flat and slice serves to each target. Keep track of the number of times you hit each target and figure out your percentage. And, as you improve, you can reduce the size of the target . . . using, say, a racquet cover or a ball can.

This target practice for the serve does a couple of things. It builds your confidence. And it tells you which serves and placements can be relied on most in a match.

PRACTICE
BY THE BOOK

For many players, conditioning is something that's a real turn-off . . . like taking out the garbage or balancing the checkbook. But it's something that has to be done if you're going to get the most out of the game.

And it doesn't need to be tedious or debilitating to be effective. All you need to do is to practice by the book.

In other words, put the cover on your racquet and slip a small book or two inside the cover next to the strings.

Then, with the books in place, practice all your strokes. Practice your swing for the serve. Practice your forehands and backhands and volleys. You can do it almost anywhere, at almost any time.

Swinging a covered racquet with a book or two inside will strengthen exactly those arm and shoulder muscles you use most on the court. You'll have two things going for you. The added weight of the books at the head of the racquet. And the greater air resistance created by the cover.

To get your muscles in shape, practice swinging by the book.

DRESS UP YOUR STROKES IN FRONT OF MIRROR

If you're having a problem getting a natural, flowing motion on a certain stroke, there's a handy way you can attack the problem right at home. That's to practice the stroke in front of a full-length mirror.

Spend about five minutes a day in front of the mirror and simulate hitting the stroke the way you'd like to be seen hitting it. Watch yourself in the mirror carefully. In two or three weeks, you should have grooved a graceful stroke this way.

At the same time, you'll create a mental image of yourself hitting that stroke the way you should. Then, the next time you're on the court and you're having trouble with your swing, try to recall that image. It should help you get your swing back on the track.

So use a full-length mirror to dress up your tennis game.

SPRINT
FOR BETTER PLAY

Bjorn Borg has remarked that a tennis match isn't a marathon run. It's a thousand 10-yard races. In other words, it's a game that requires lots of sudden, short bursts of speed.

Now there's no question that jogging a mile or more a few times a week will help your game. It'll help give you the stamina you need to hang tough in a long match.

But if you're in reasonably good shape already, there's another kind of running that's even more valuable. And that's doing wind sprints.

Wind sprints are a series of short dashes during which you run all-out . . . pause . . . and then go full-blast again. An easy way to do wind sprints is to dash the length of a court along the sideline. Do a series of dashes for as long as you can, and build up the number gradually.

It will improve your quickness. And if you do enough wind sprints, of course, it builds your endurance, too . . . just like jogging.

Bjorn Borg

HIT OUT
TO GET DEPTH

If too many of your shots land short in the other court . . . where your opponents can pick them off for easy winners . . . the best way to conquer the problem is to practice hitting balls too deep.

On conventional forehands and backhands, try hitting past the baseline for a time during a practice session. You'll soon get the feel of long drives, and you can begin gradually to shorten them until they're landing just inside the baseline.

The same principle applies to lobs. If you've been sending up lobs that are too short, start trying to hit the baseline with them when you're practicing. Imagine that there are ball cans along the line, and that you are aiming to knock the cans over.

And don't worry that you'll get into the habit of hitting groundstrokes and lobs out during your actual matches. In competition, you'll naturally tend to hit shorter on all shots because you'll be a bit tighter.

So hit too deep in practice to hit deep enough when it counts.

Jimmy Connors

GET THE MOST FROM YOUR LESSONS

In order to get your money's worth from a lesson, you've got to do more than just show up on time. Teaching pros say there are three things that are especially important: conditioning, a little advance planning and practice.

You've got to be in fairly good physical shape to get the most out of a lesson. So do some regular exercising.

Second, have a definite idea of what you'd like to work on when you arrive for a lesson. The pro may have some thoughts. But you should be able to make some suggestions, too. After all, you know your strengths and weaknesses better than anybody.

Third, you've got to practice between lessons. Most pros say that the best practice-to-lesson ratio is about five-to-one. In other words, if you take a half-hour lesson each week, you should spend about two and a half hours a week practicing what you've learned.

Otherwise, you won't absorb what you've been taught. And if you don't do that, of course, you won't improve. Which is why you're taking lessons in the first place, isn't it?

PROFIT FROM PRACTICE WITH WEAKER PLAYERS

If you find yourself across the net from a considerably weaker player, it's still possible to make the match interesting and fun.

All you have to do is agree ahead of time on a few pre-set conditions that will bring out the best in you.

One way to do that is to give your opponent a handicap. You can start every game at love-30 in his favor, for instance.

You'll be amazed at how that will focus your concentration. You will have to bear down and make every shot count, because every point has suddenly become a big one.

There are other ways to have an interesting match with a weaker player. You can try to hit every shot to a given spot. Or you can work on those tough shots hit in no-man's land, that awkward area between the baseline and the service line. The possibilities are endless.

You don't want to play against weaker opponents all the time, of course. But when you do, you can make it interesting and fun. Give yourself a handicap, for example, or deliberately practice those tough shots you need to improve.

SHARPEN YOUR CONCENTRATION

You can practice your groundstrokes and serves and volleys easily enough. But how do you practice your concentration?

It's easy. Just use a felt-tip marker to put a large spot on a few of your practice balls.

Then, rally with them during your practice sessions. Or use them during practice matches. And as you do, look for the spots that are revolving around the spinning balls as they cross the net.

You'll find that the marked balls will help you train yourself to focus your attention sharply on the ball. They'll also help you to learn to screen out those many distractions that can ruin your concentration. Distractions like noise from neighboring games, or car horns.

So if your concentration tends to fail you at critical spots, try solving the problem by spotting your practice balls.

Pam Shriver

ACQUIRE BALL SENSE

You've got to have ball sense to do your best on court. That means having a good fix on the true line of flight of every ball so that you'll know where it's going to bounce each time. The better your ball sense, the more quickly you'll get into position to hit shots correctly.

Can you develop ball sense? Yes, and a good way to do it is to practice groundstrokes from three feet behind the baseline. Watch balls hit by your practice partner from the moment they leave the strings. Pay special attention to the height at which the balls clear the net.

If a ball clears the net by more than three feet, it will land in the back third of your court. If a ball clears the net by under a foot, the chances are that it will land in the first third of your court. Notice this correlation in practice and it will come to you automatically during actual play.

Also, try this. Let a few balls bounce without hitting them during your practice session. Note how high the ball bounces before it begins to fall. Then, as you begin hitting, remember to bring your racquet back on the same level as the anticipated peak of each bounce.

By polishing up your ball sense in practice, you'll really sharpen your instincts for your actual matches.